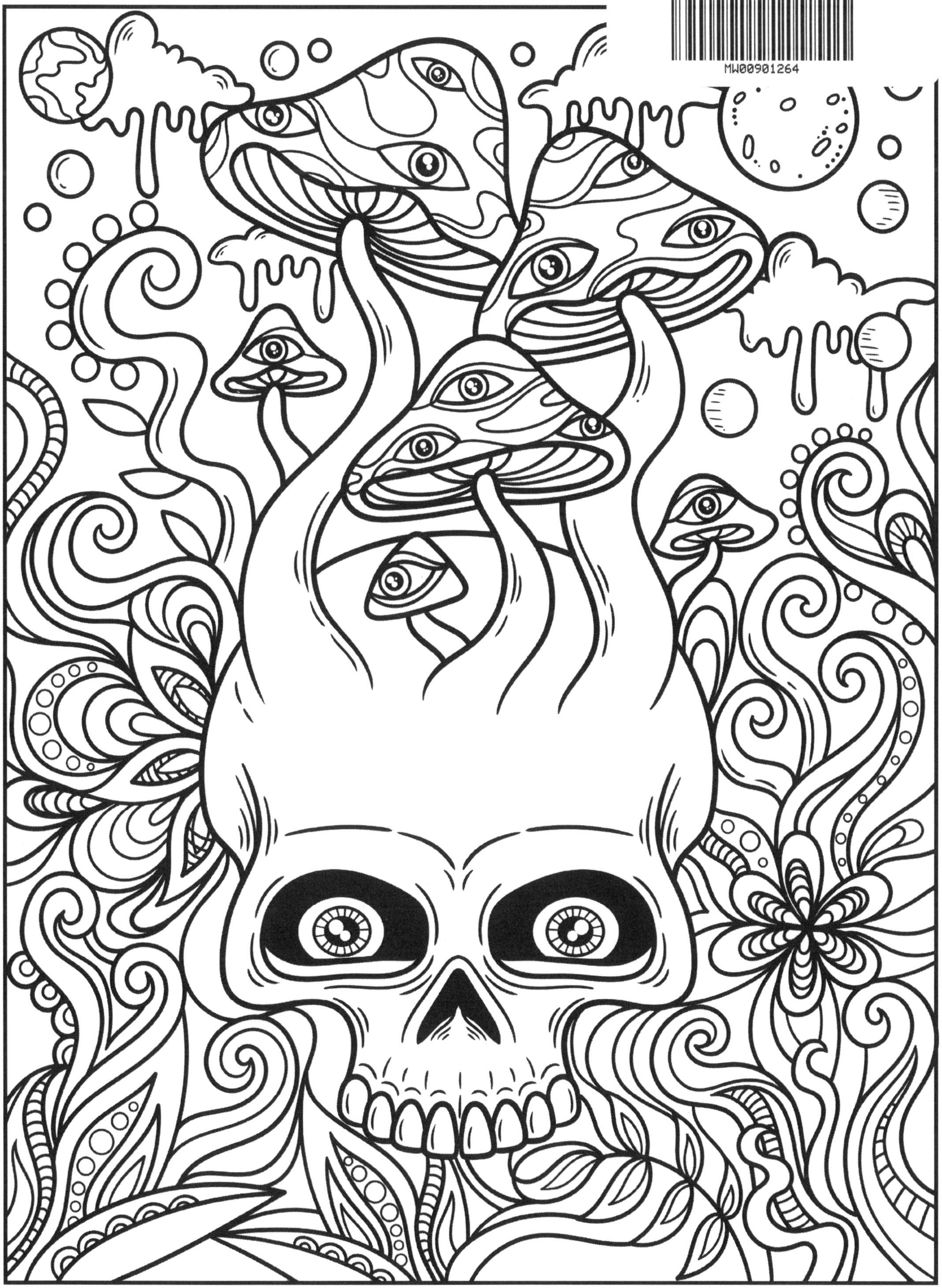

Art by : Leriza May Marinãs

First edition: 2020

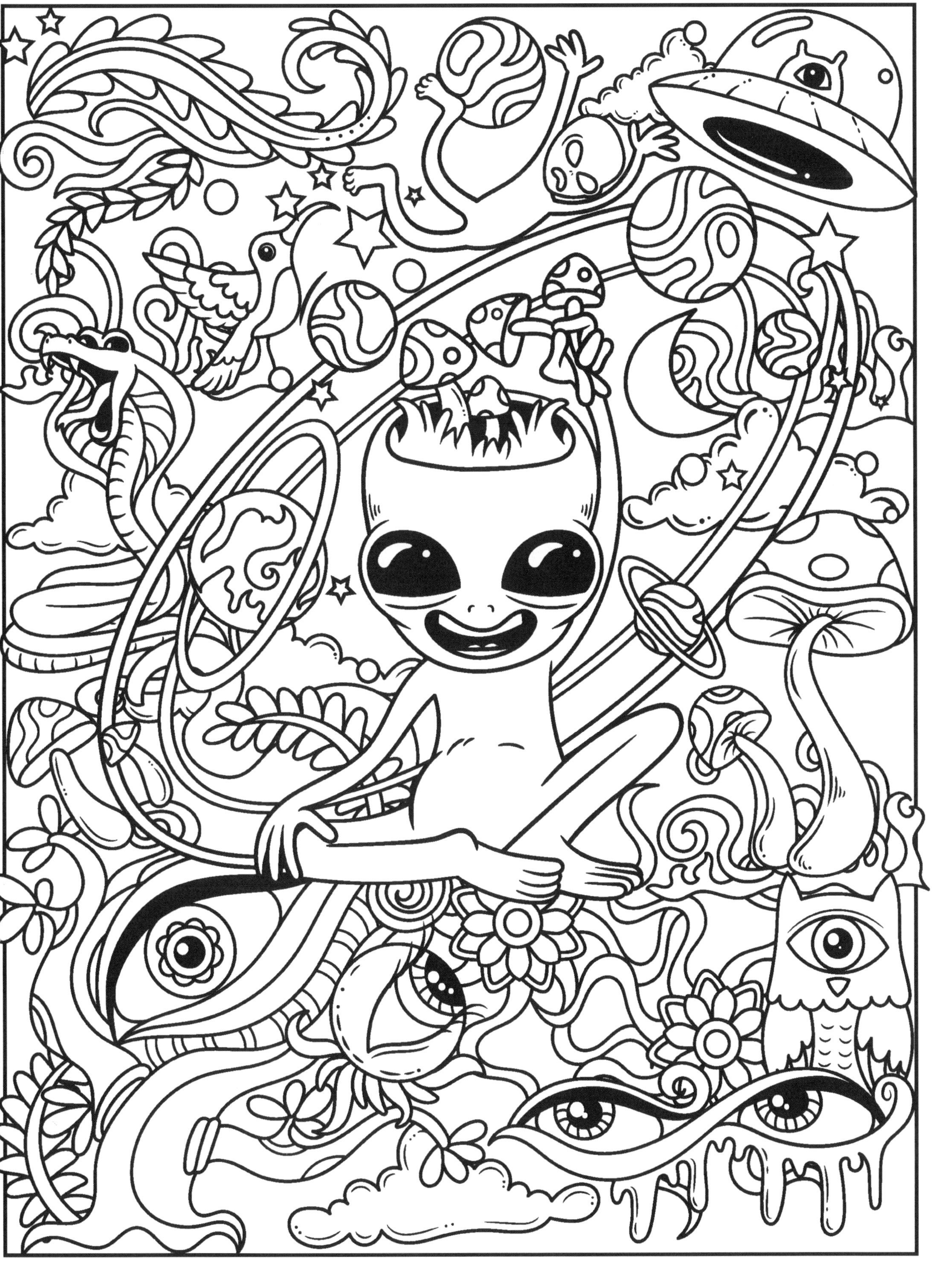

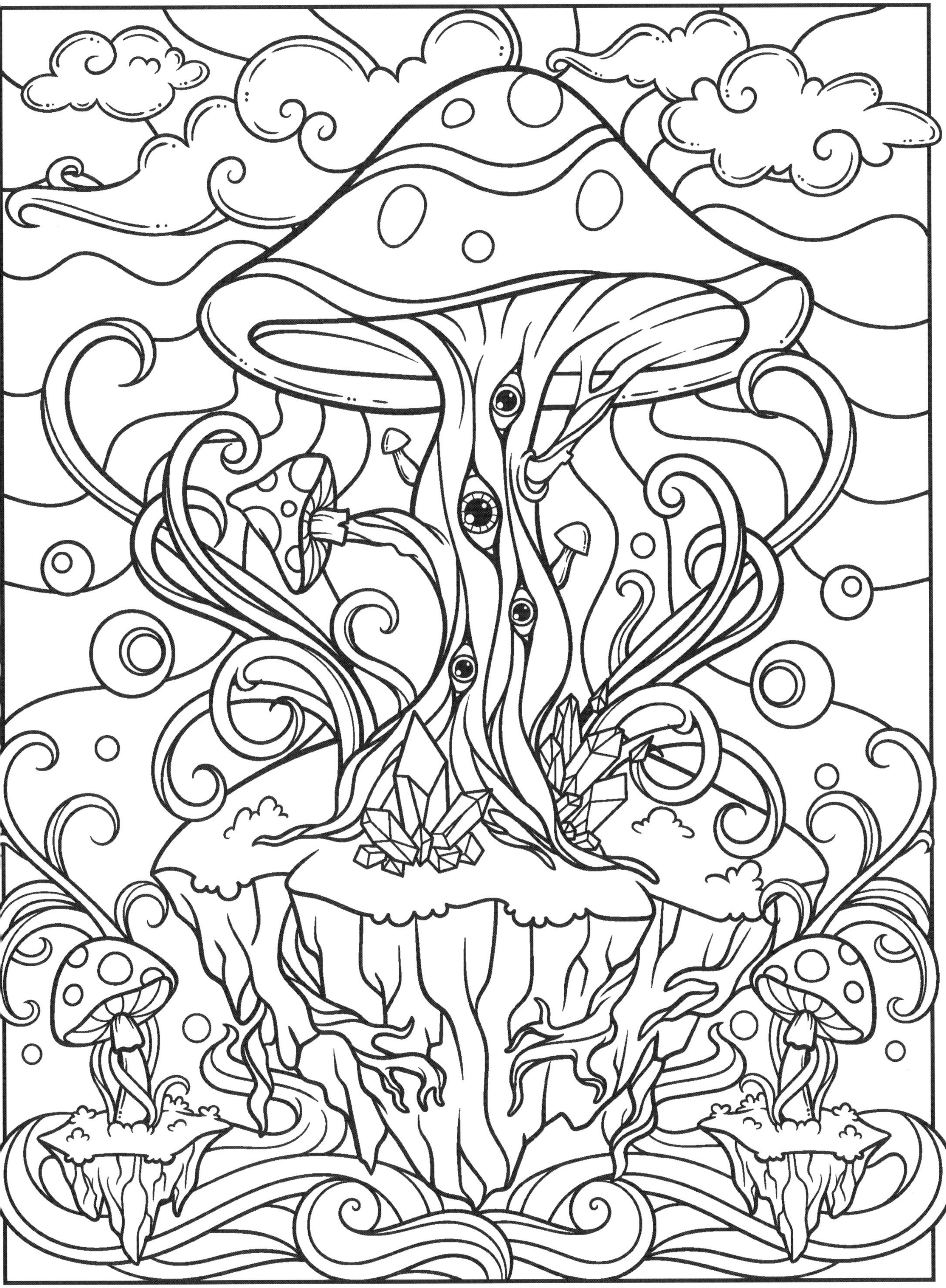

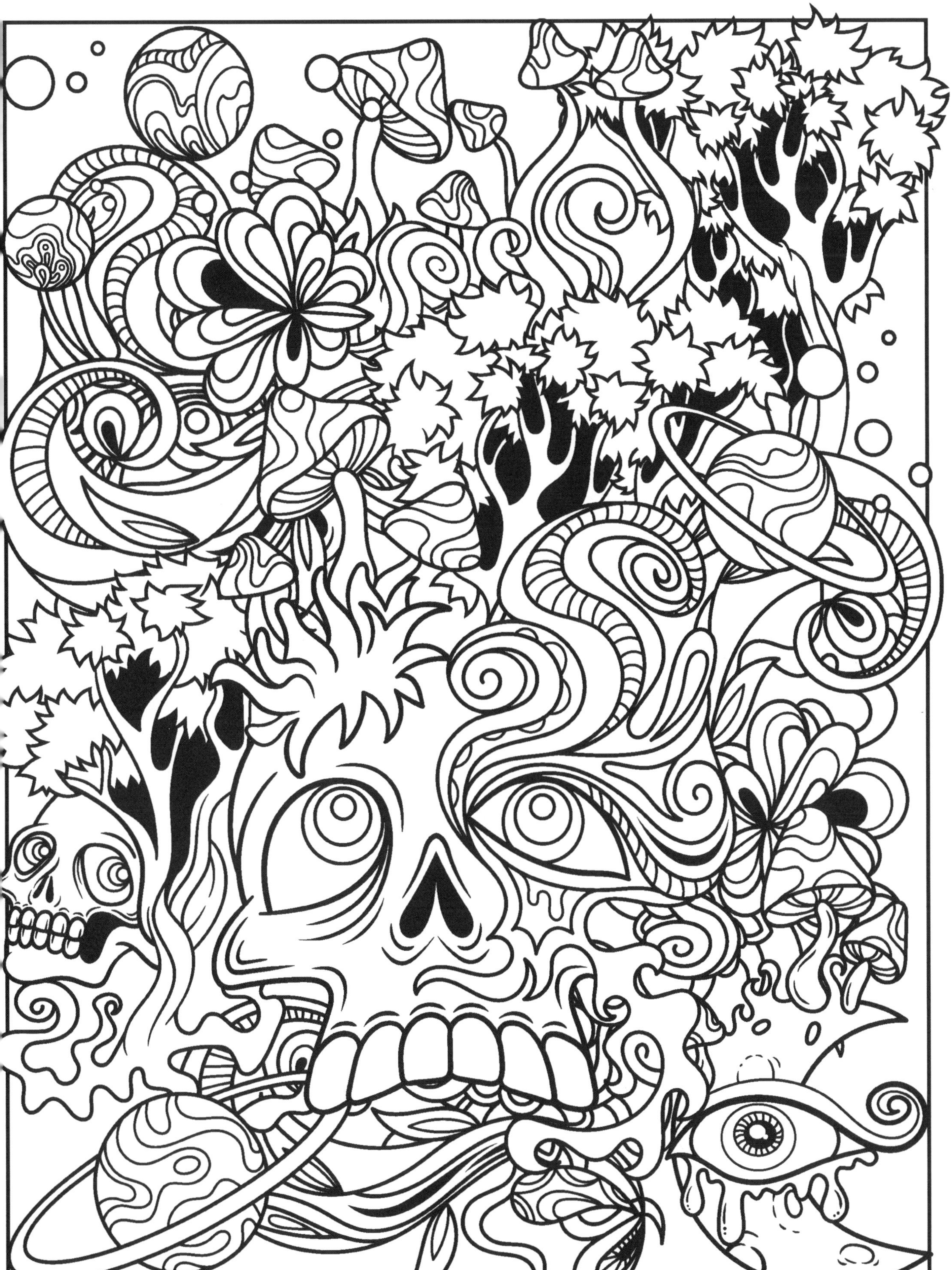

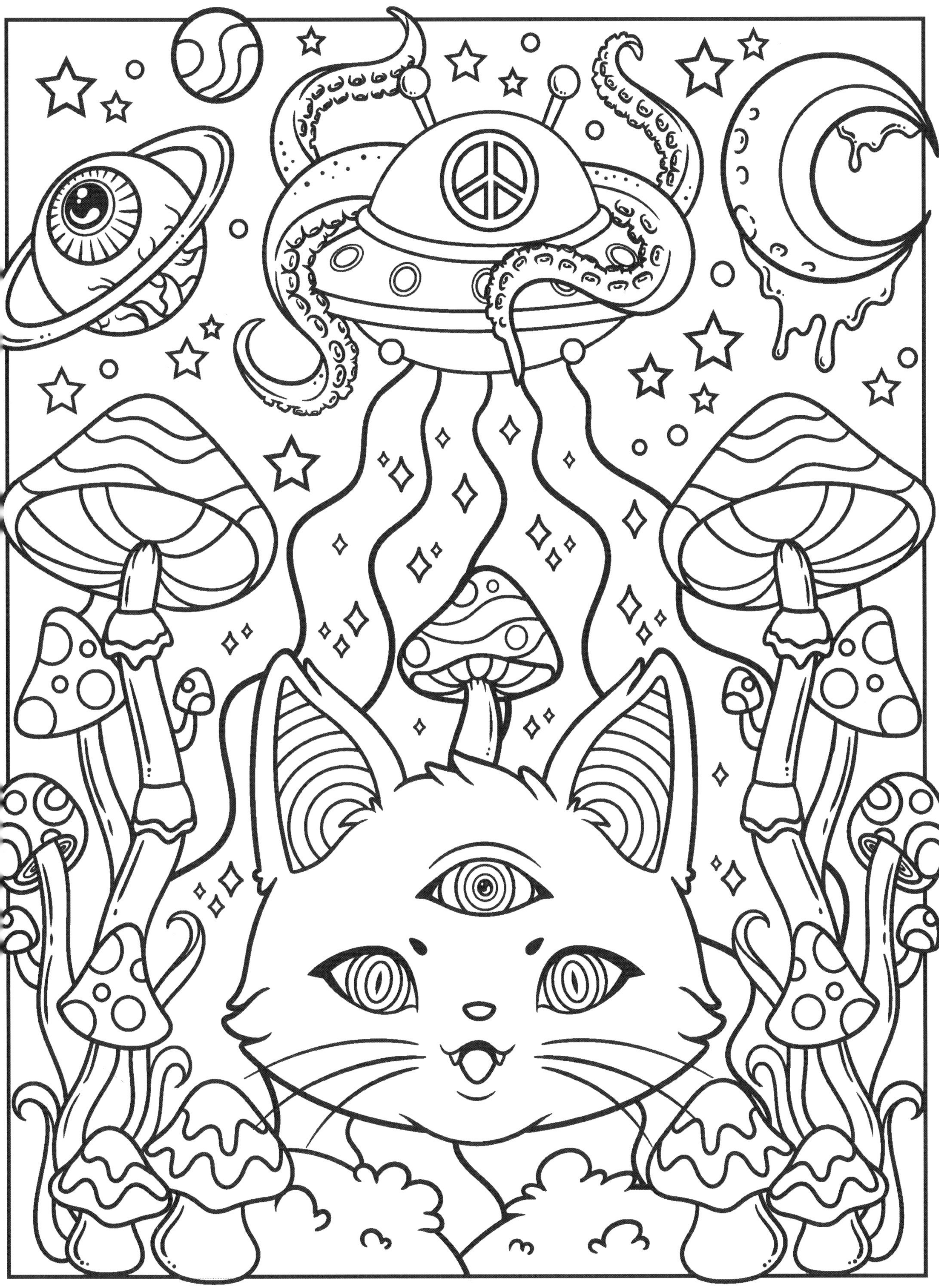

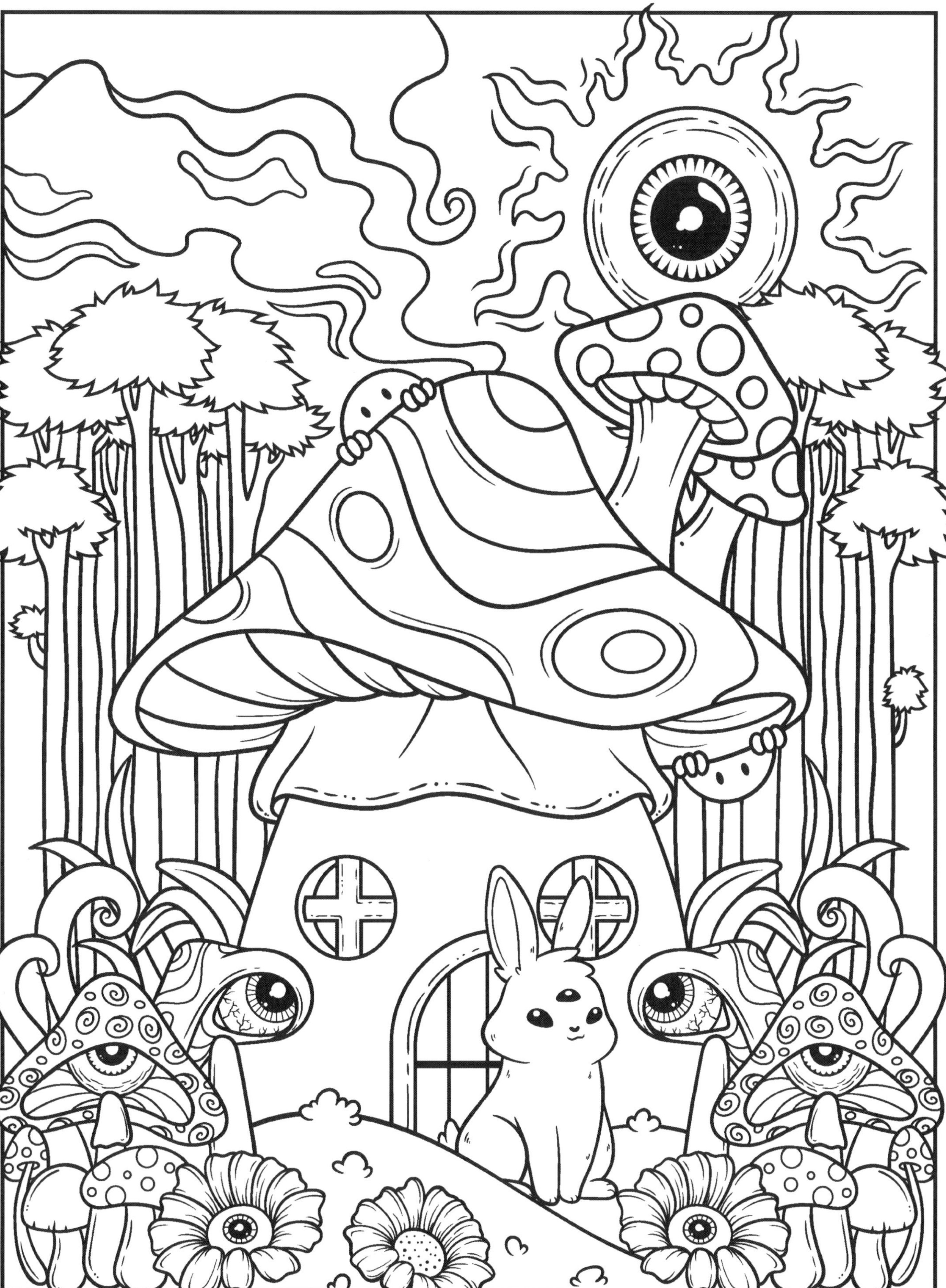

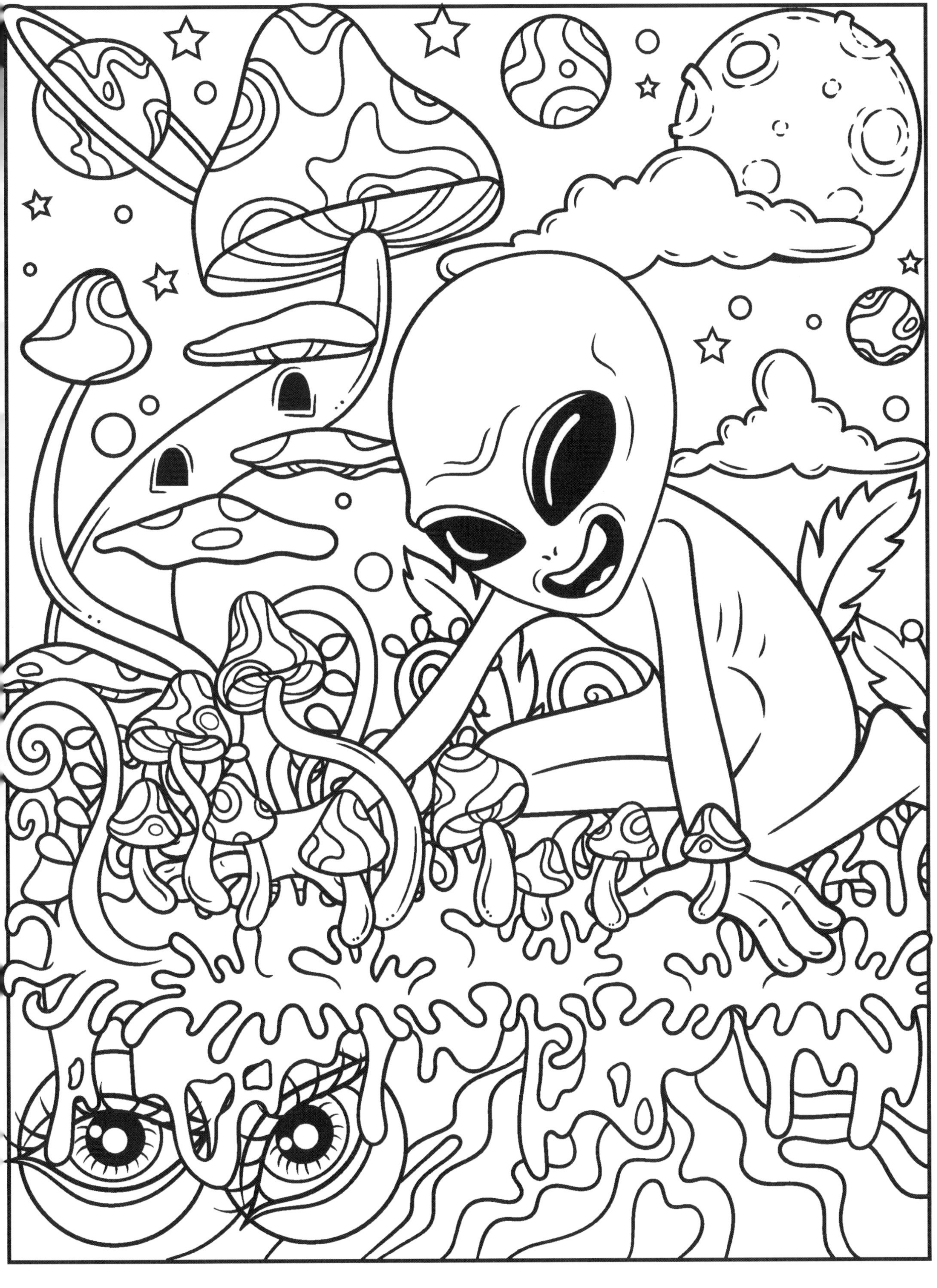

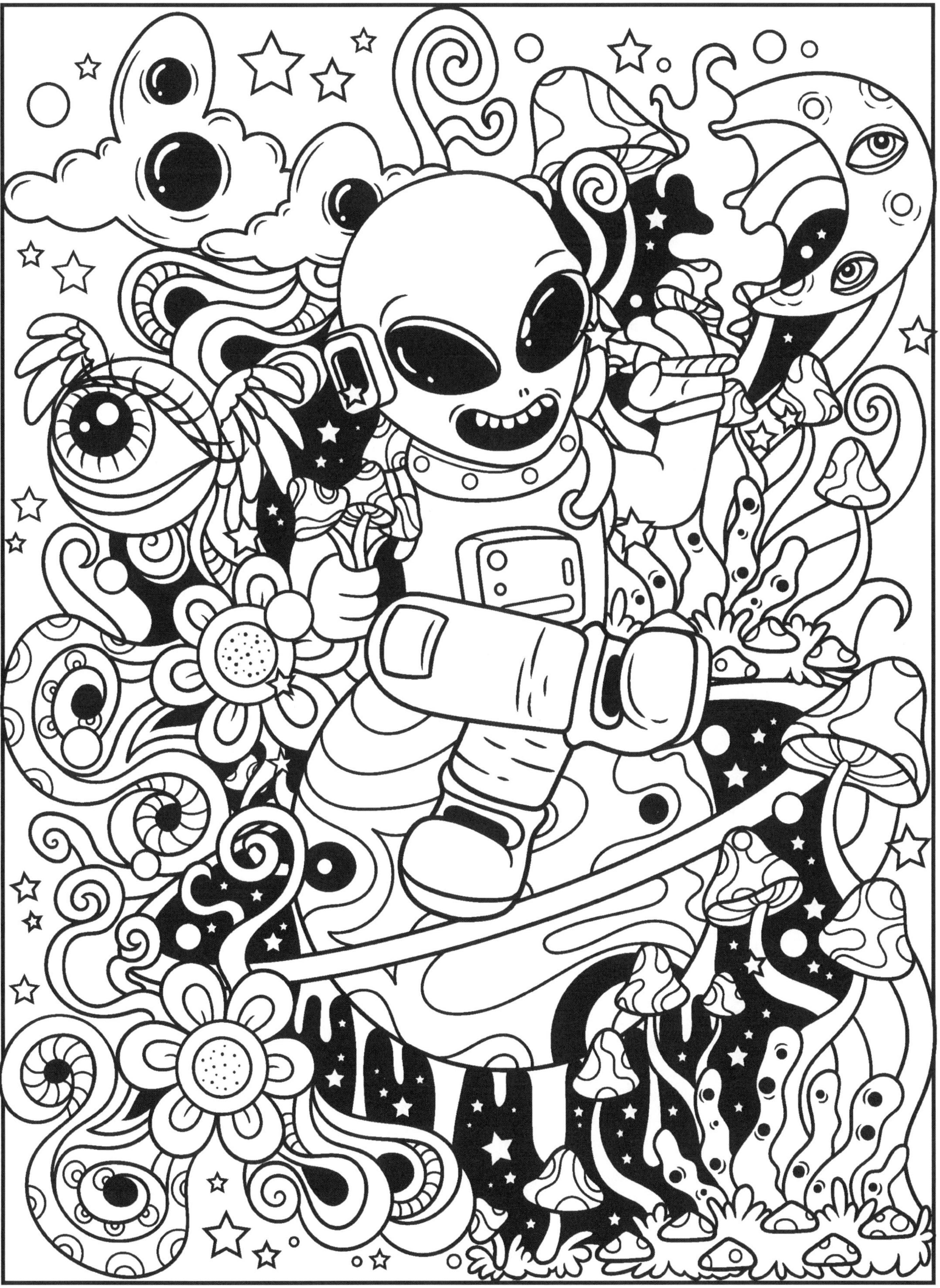

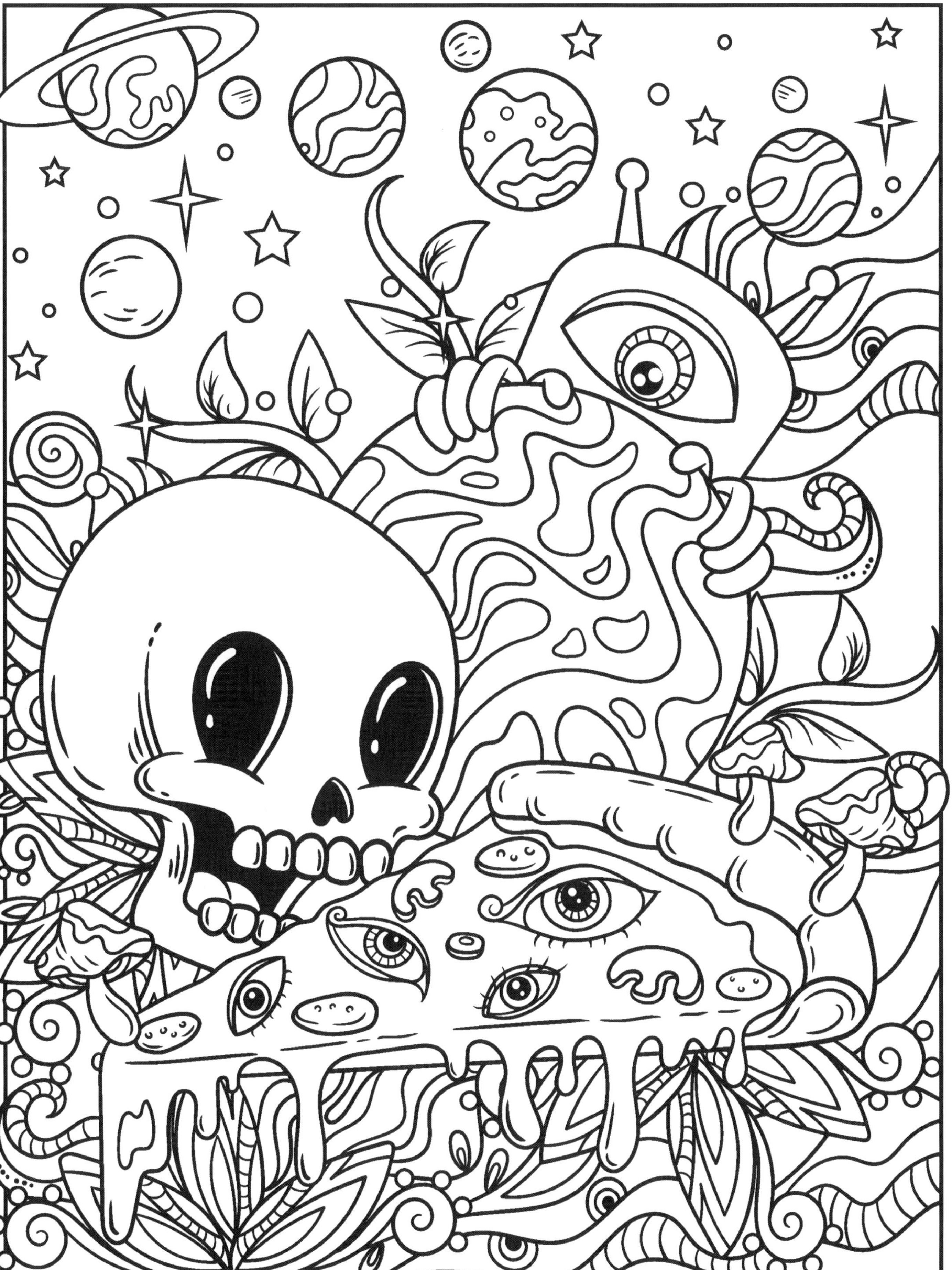

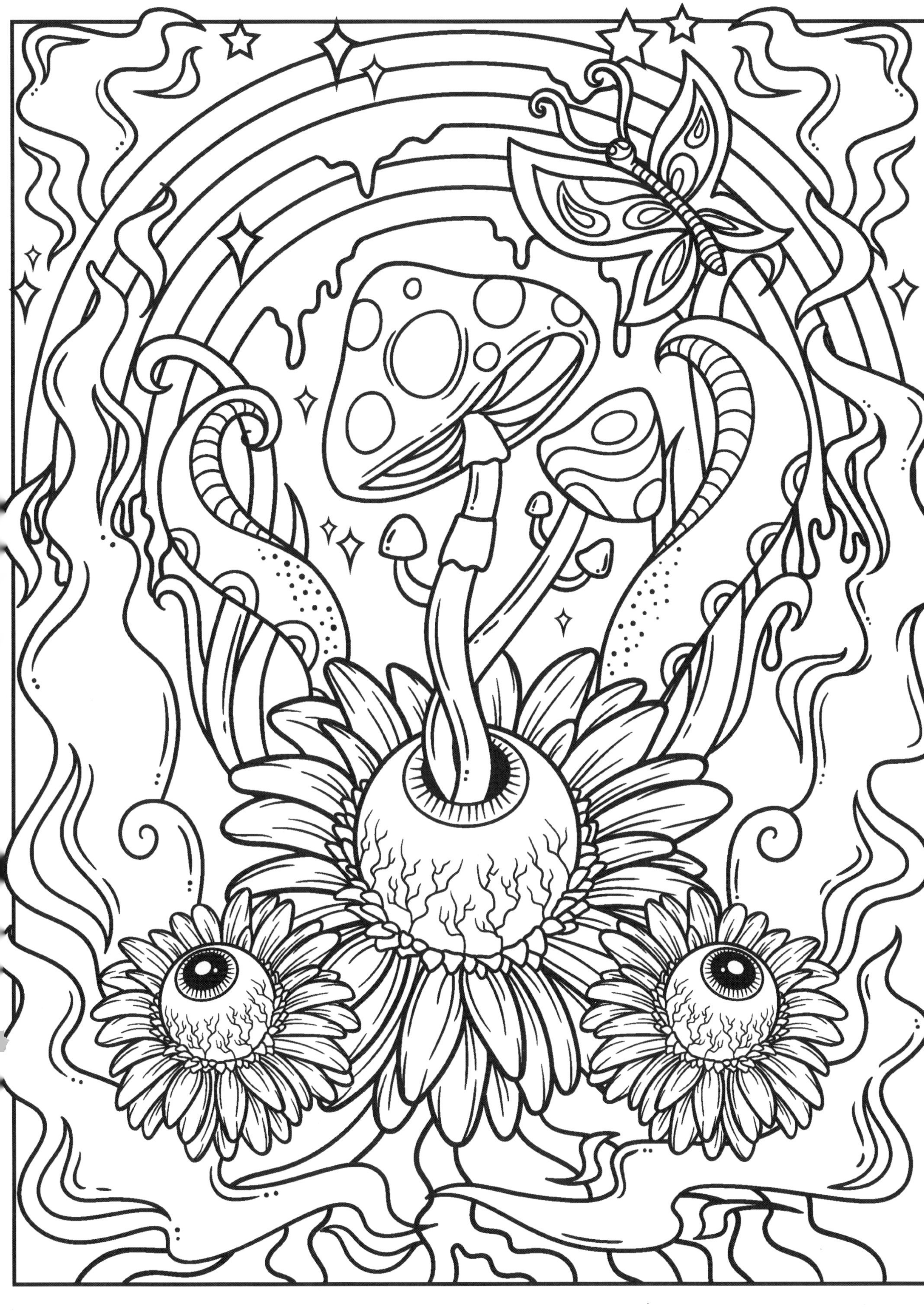

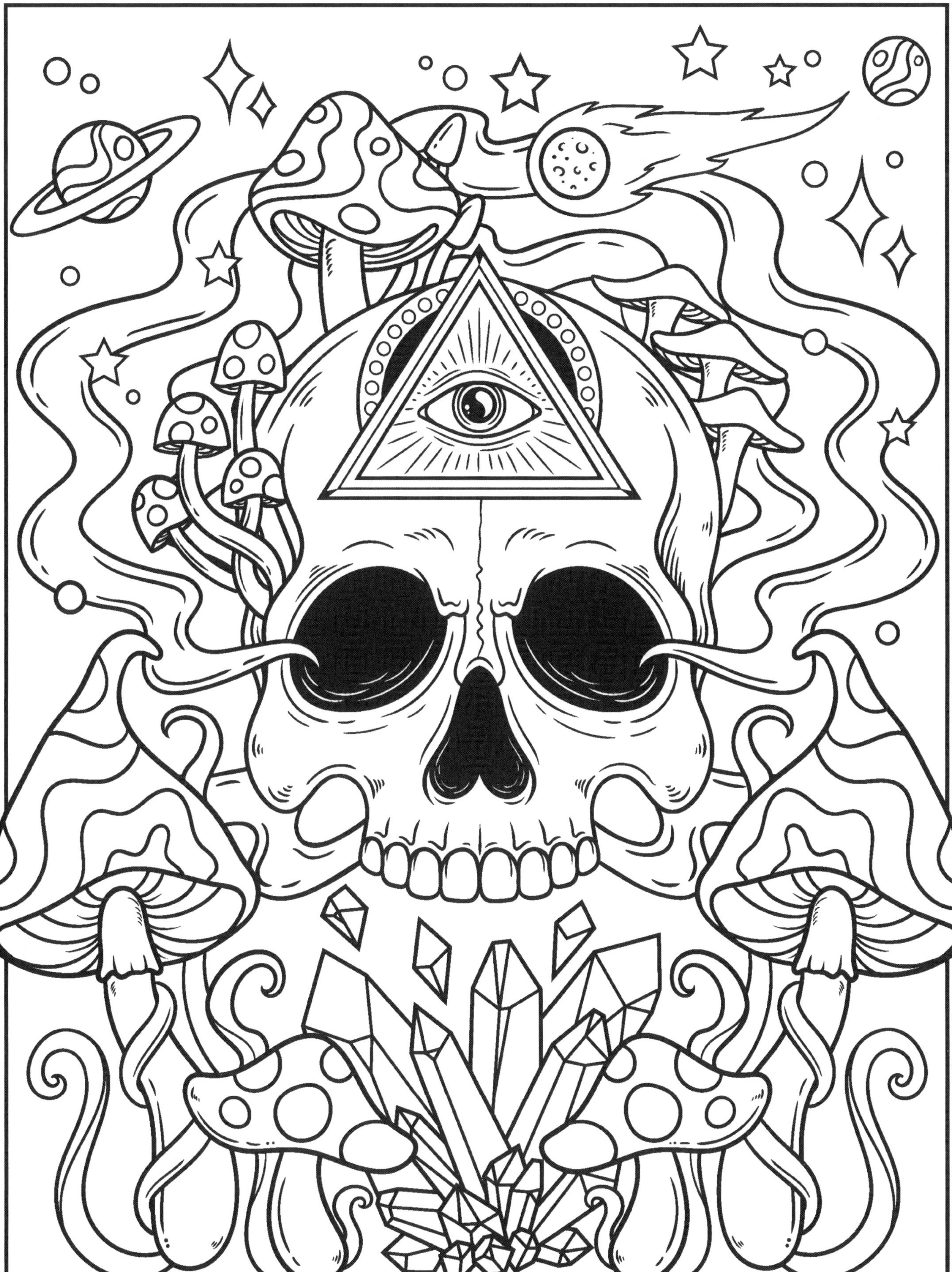

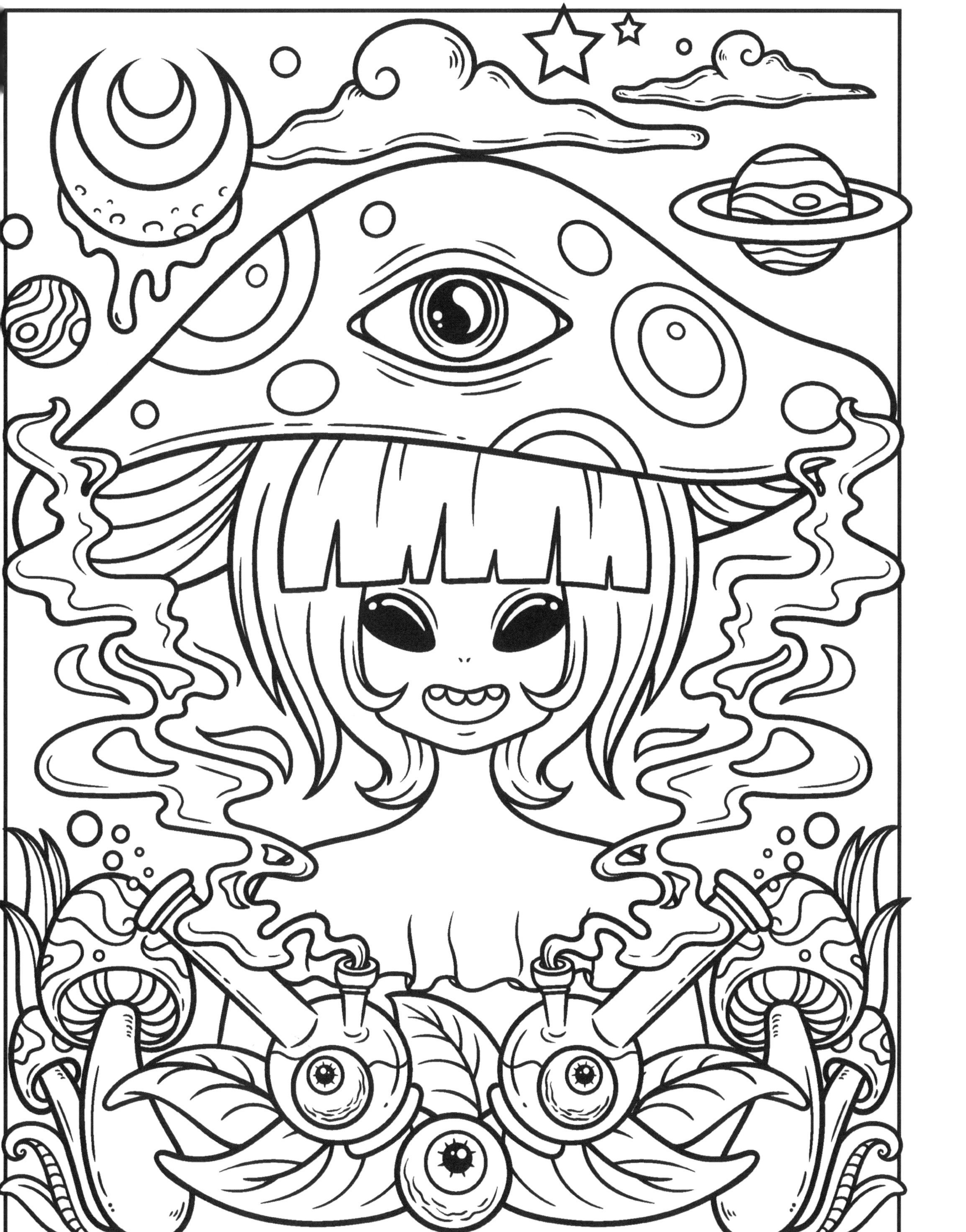

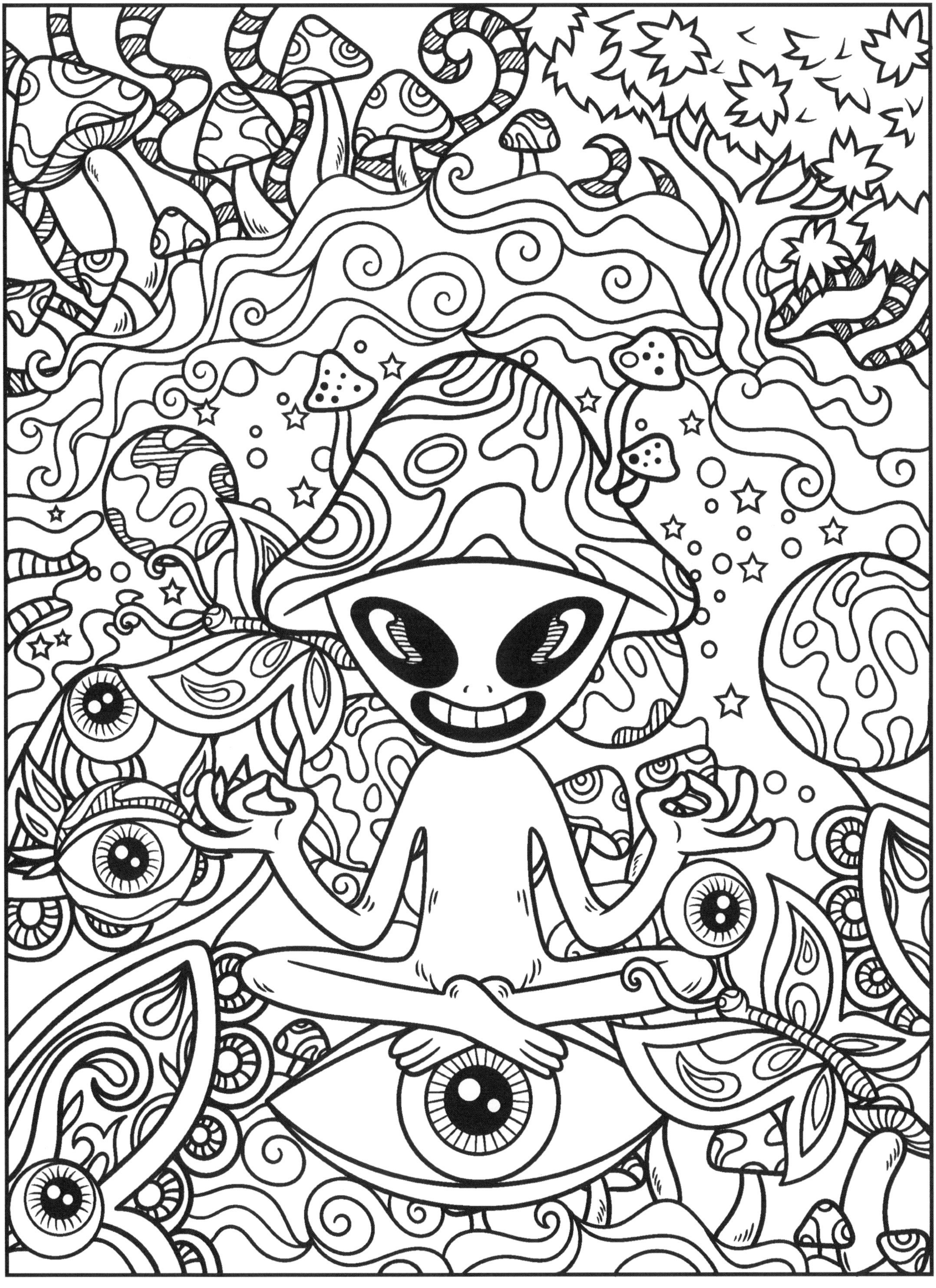

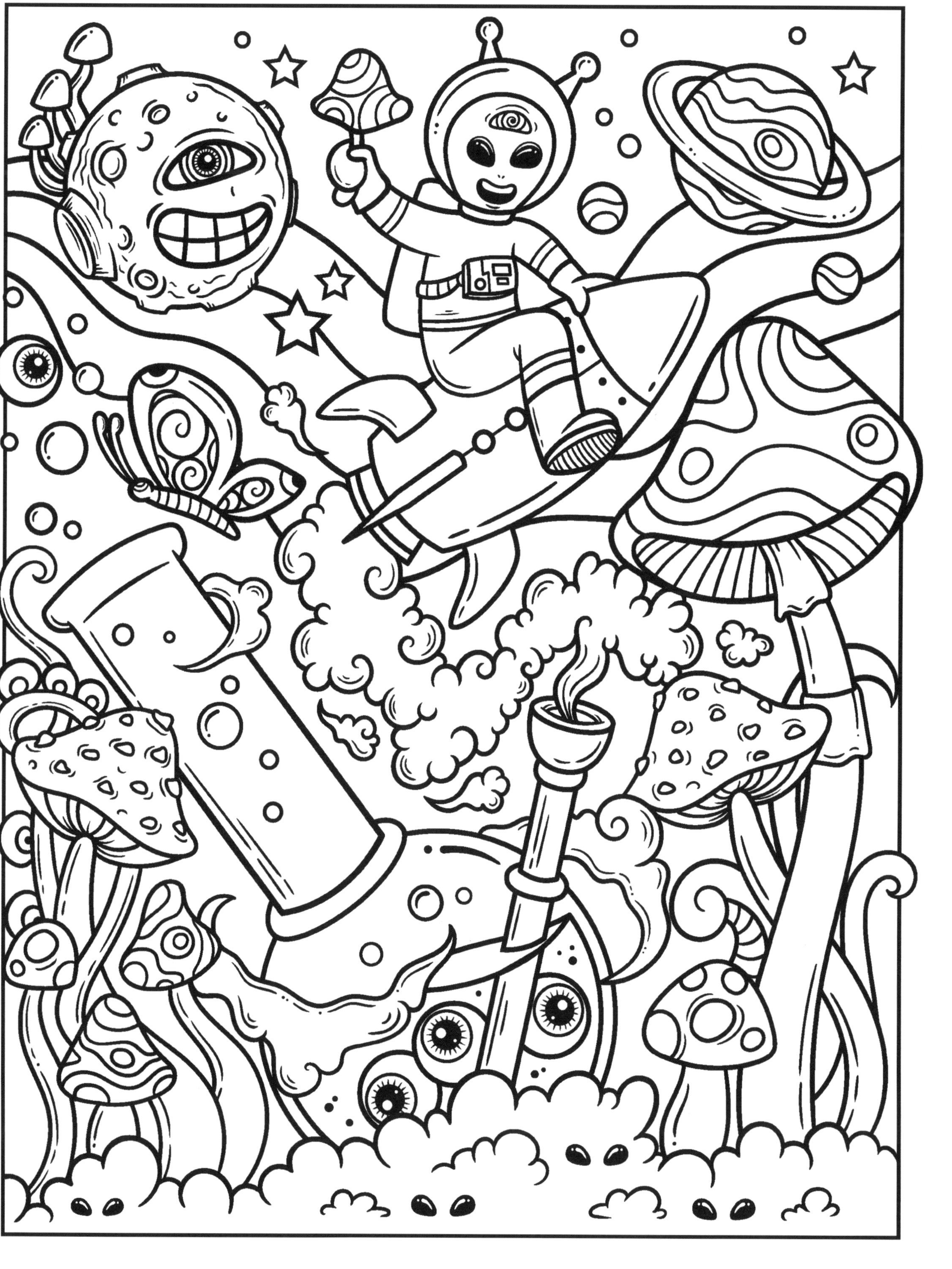

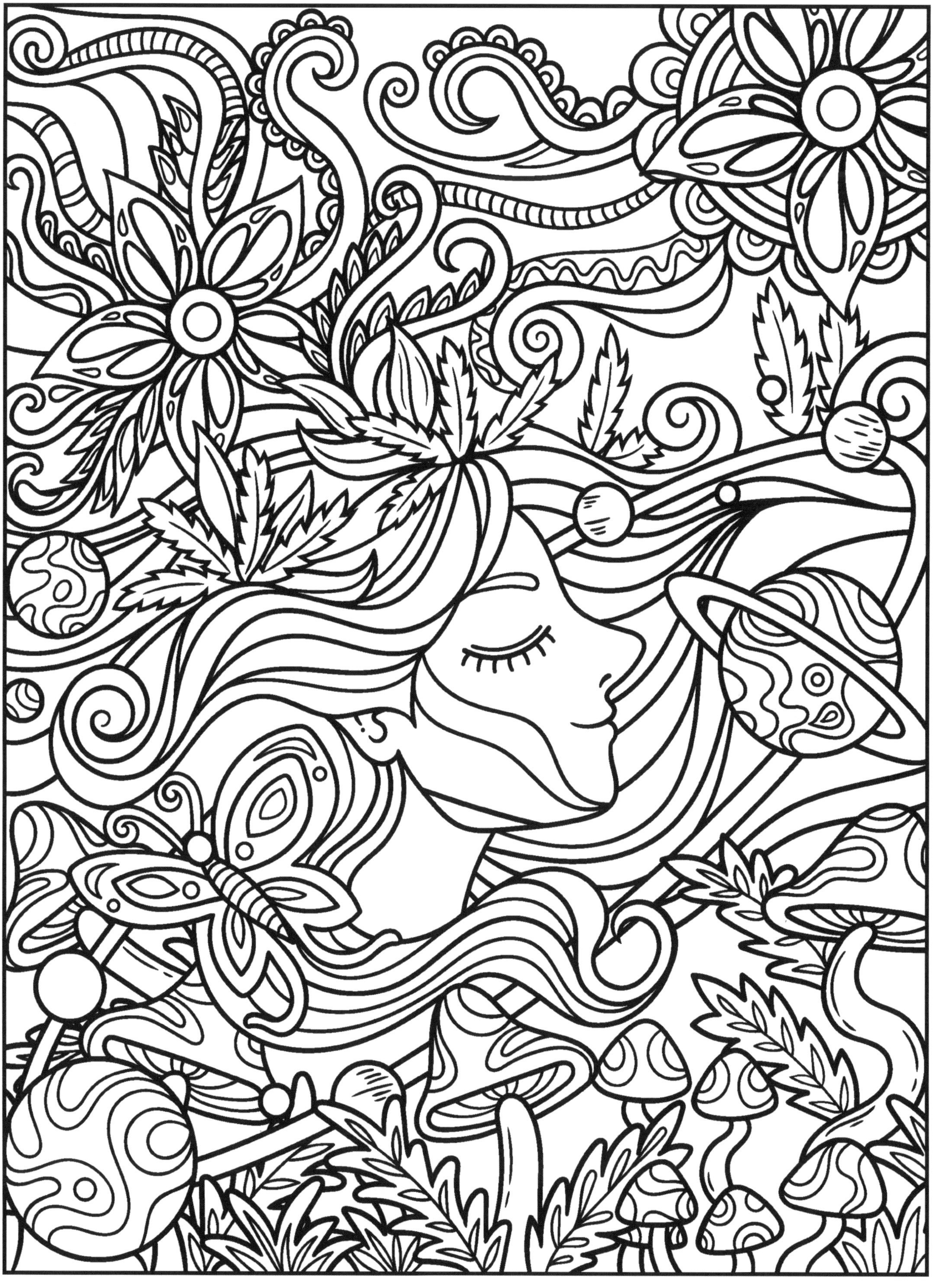

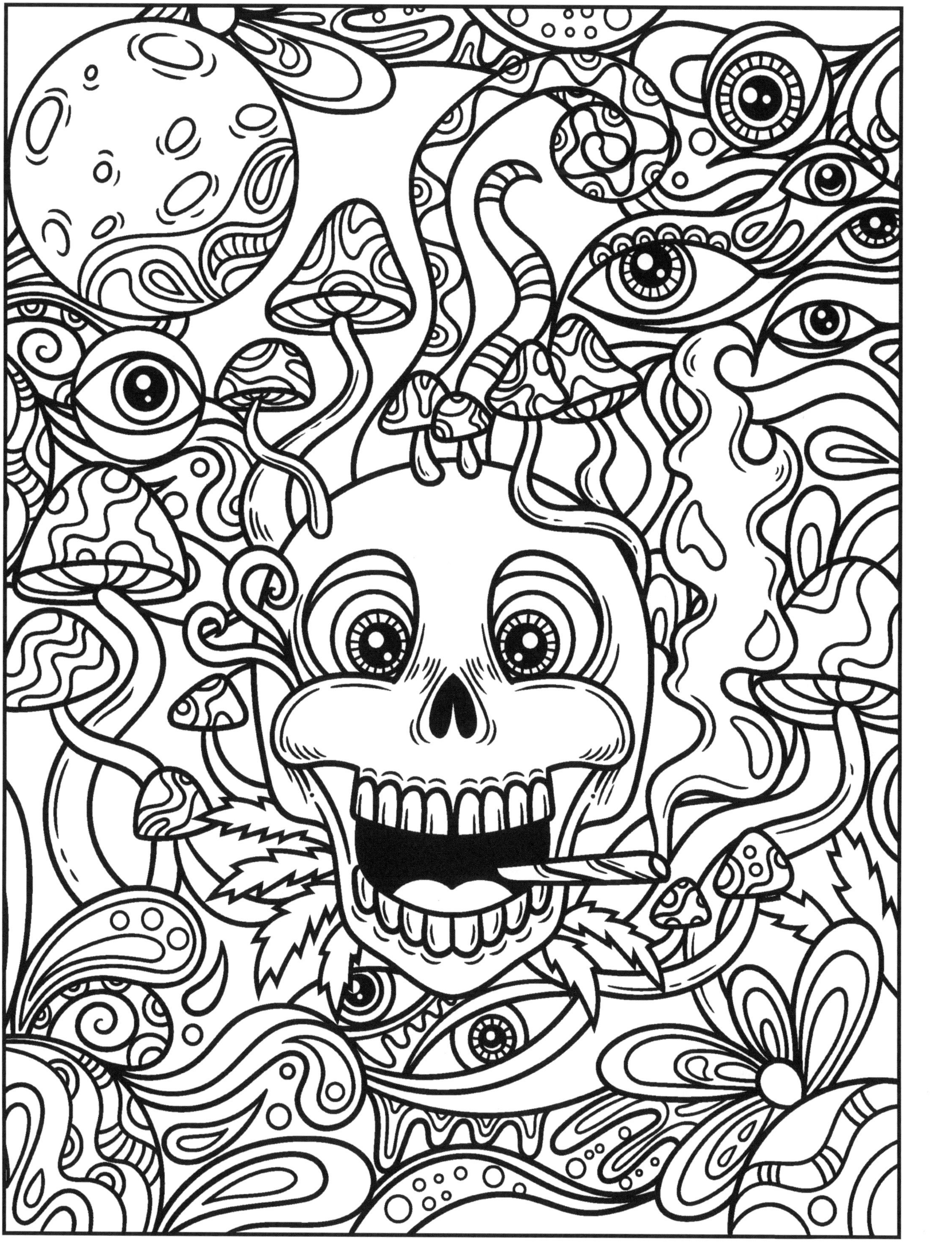

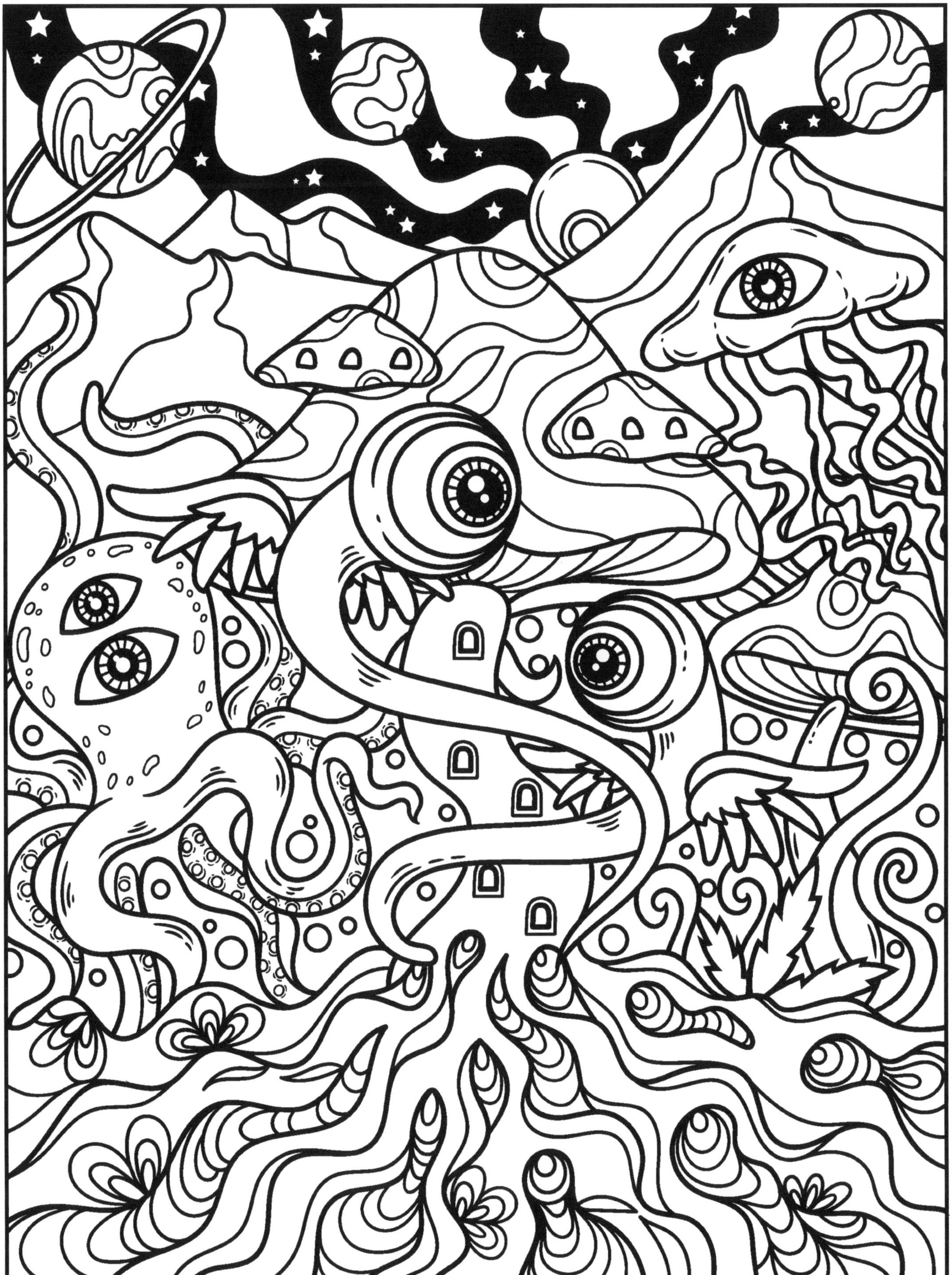

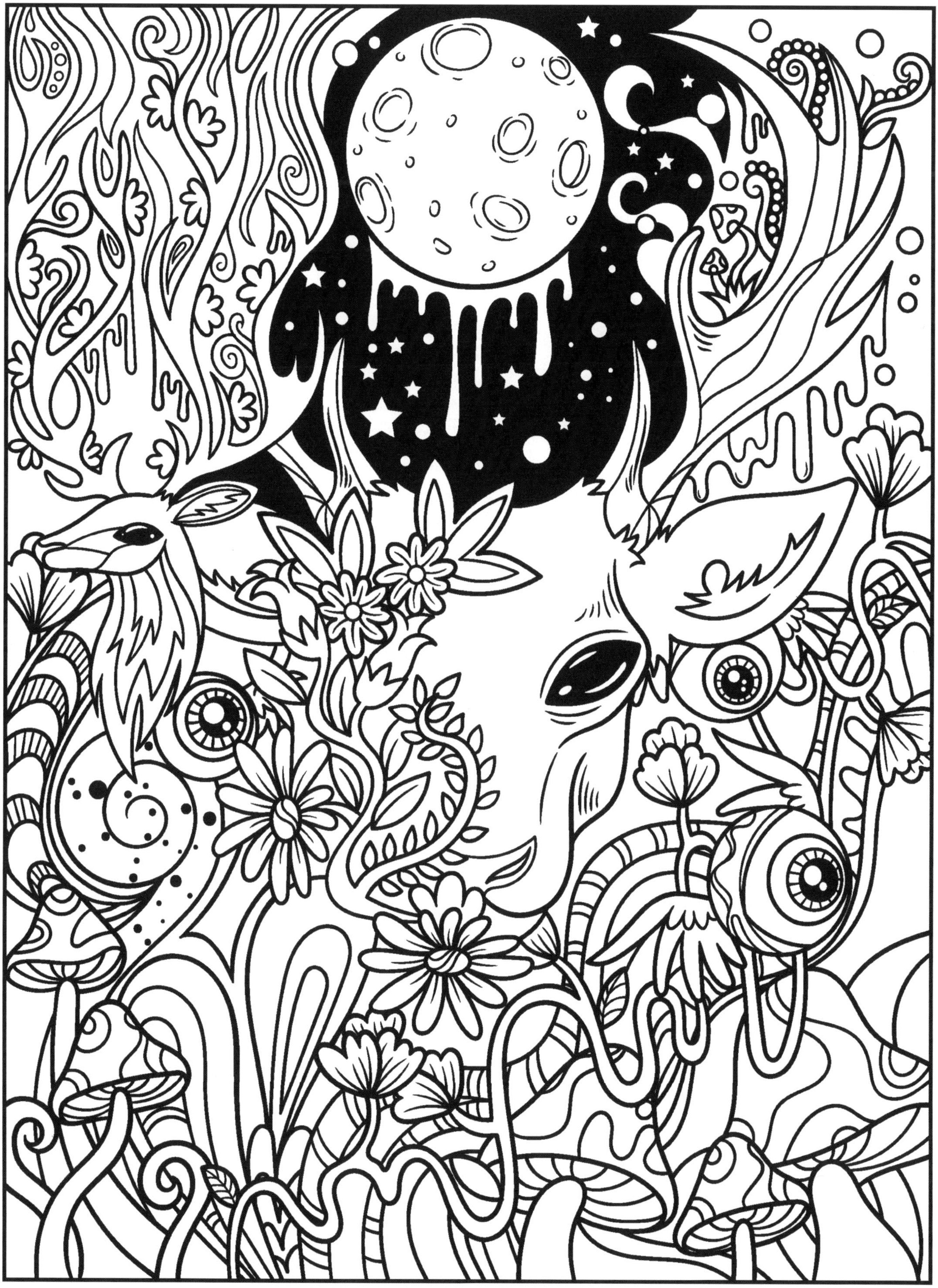

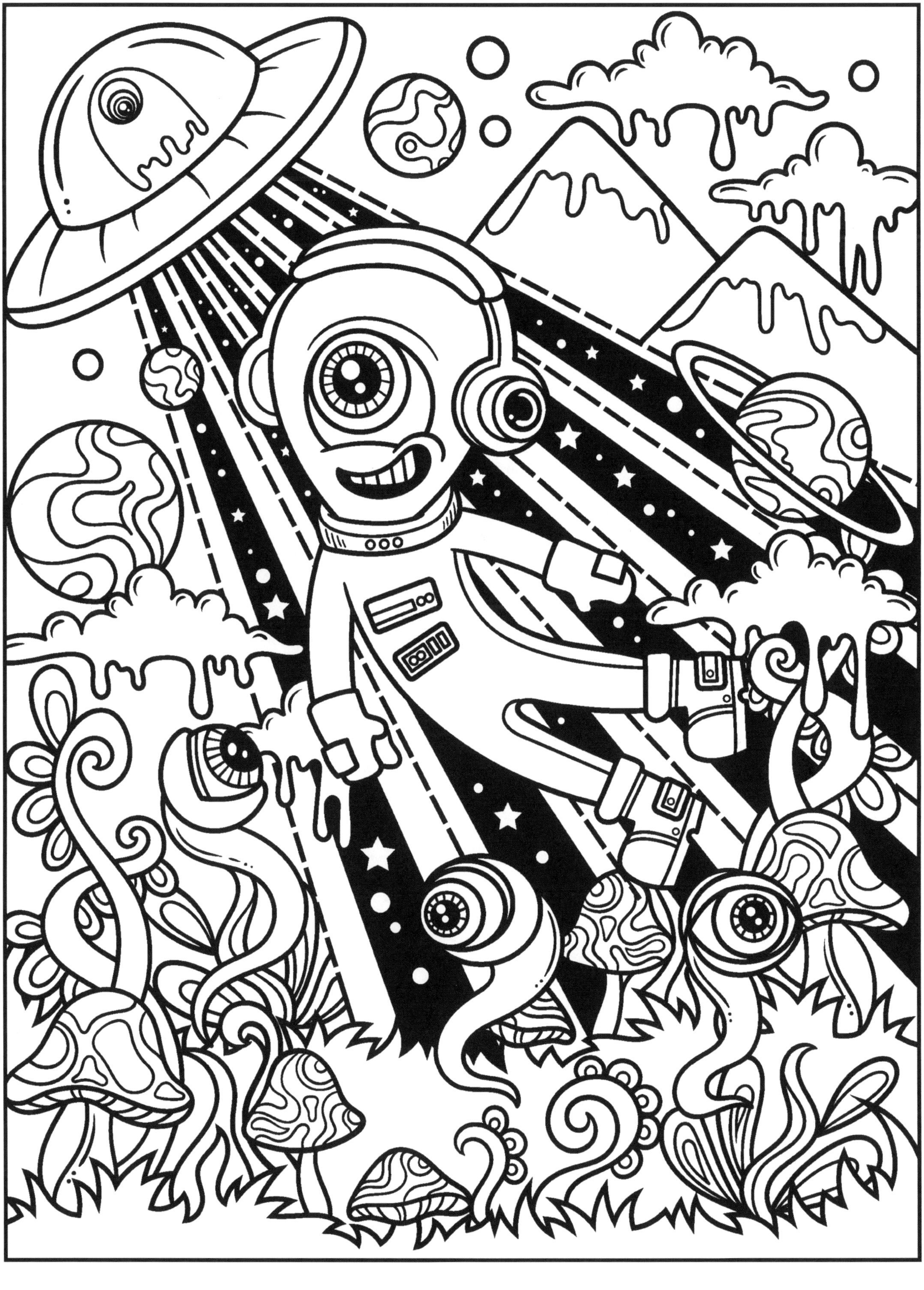

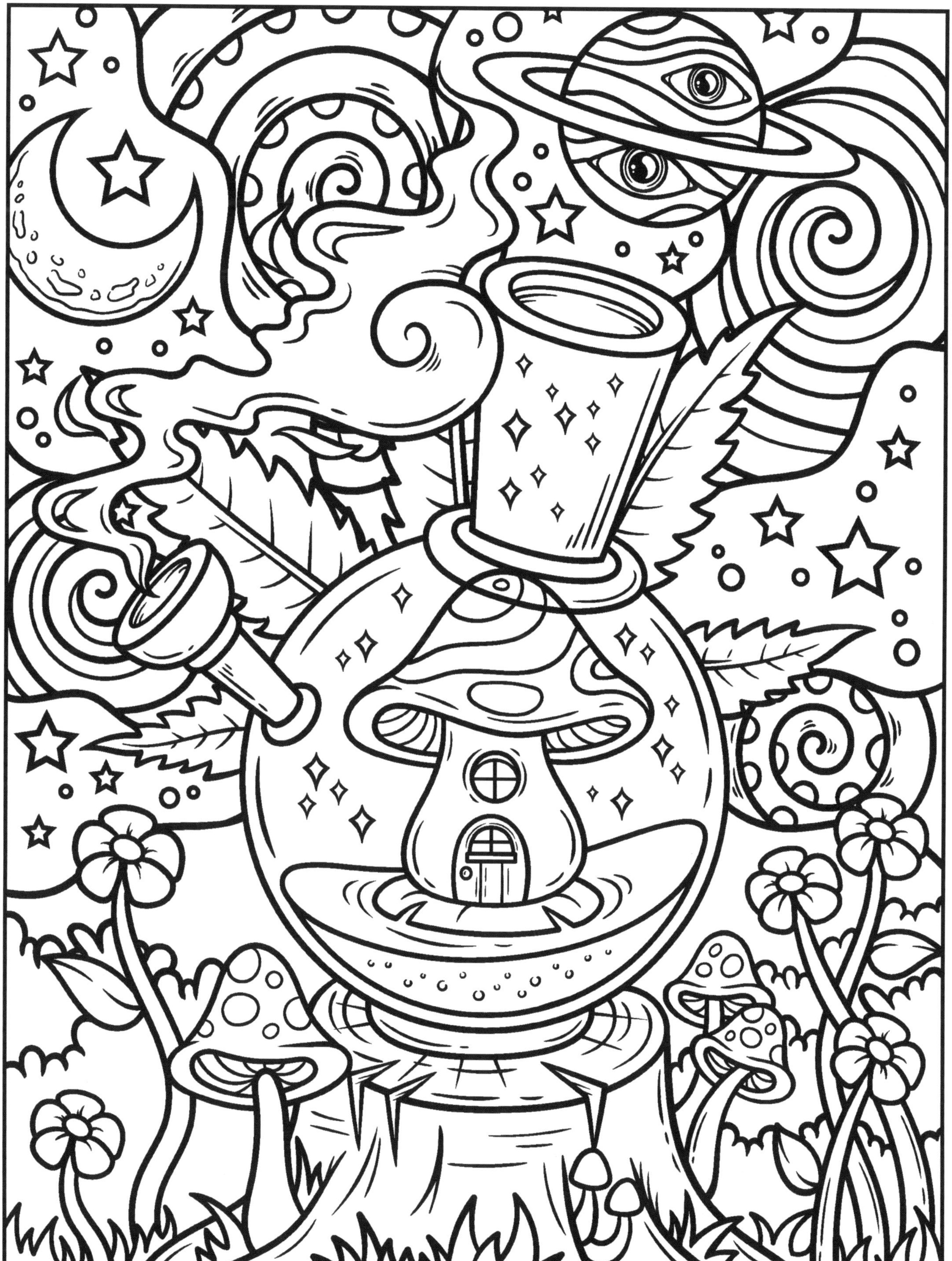

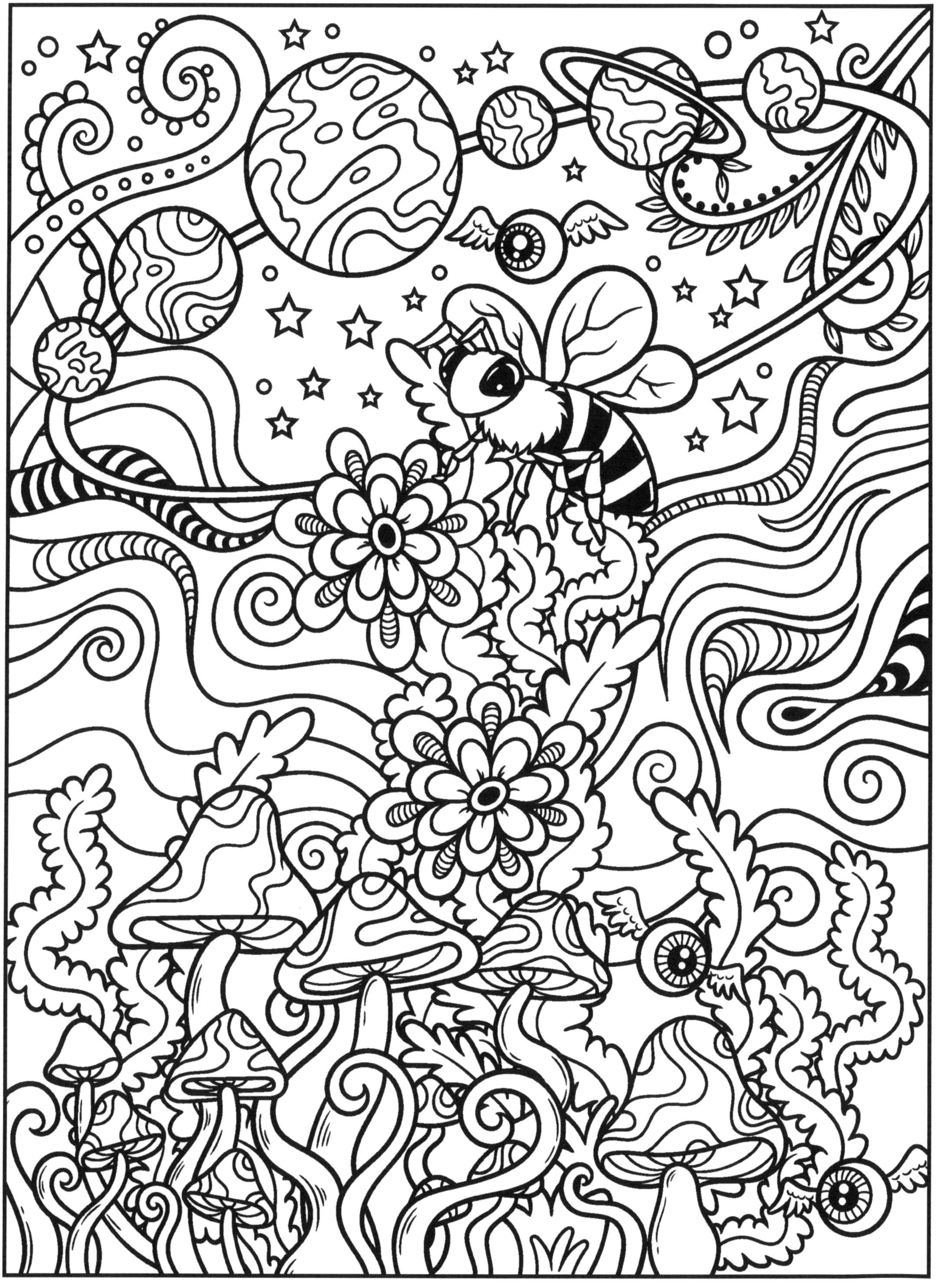

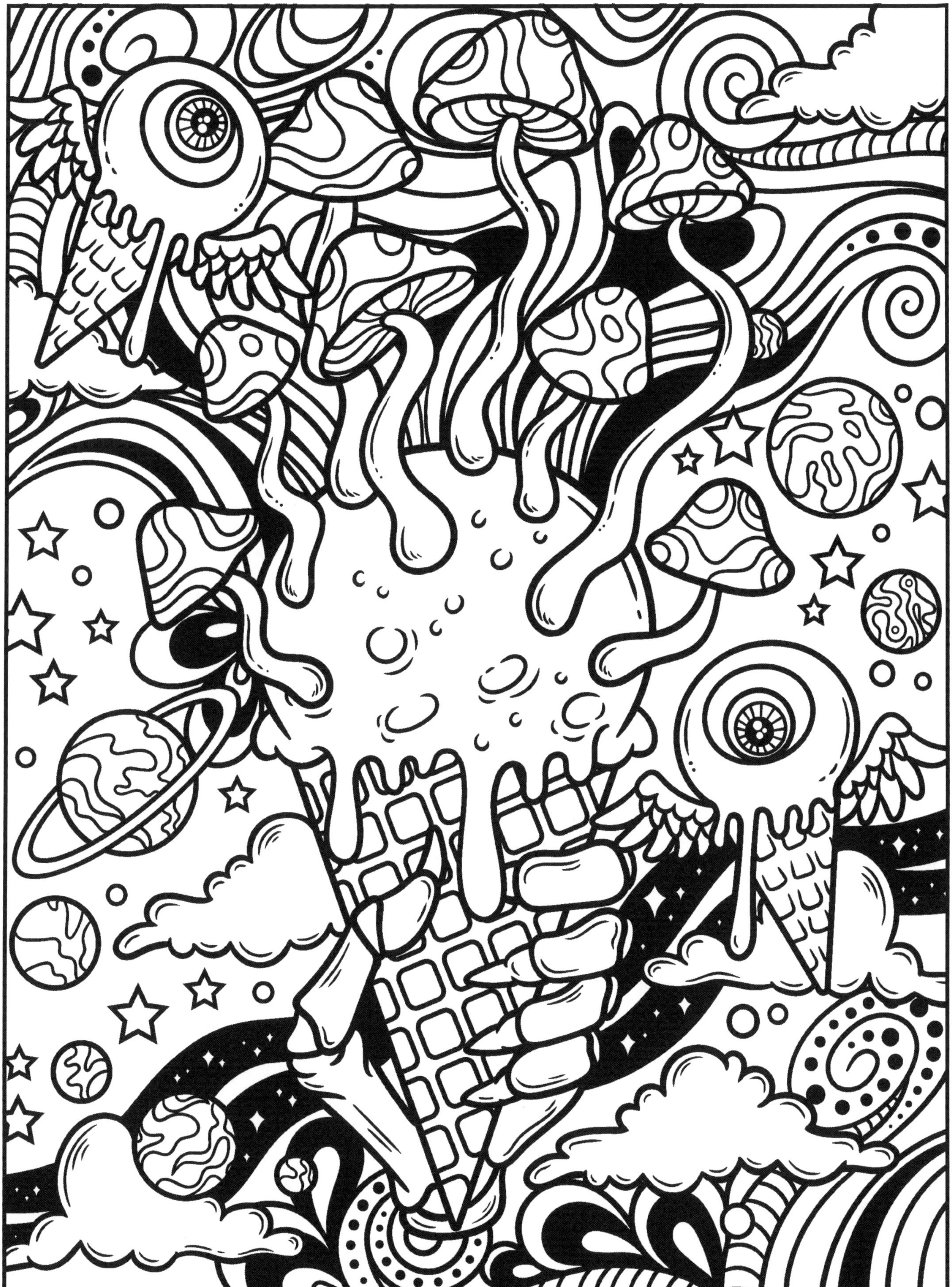

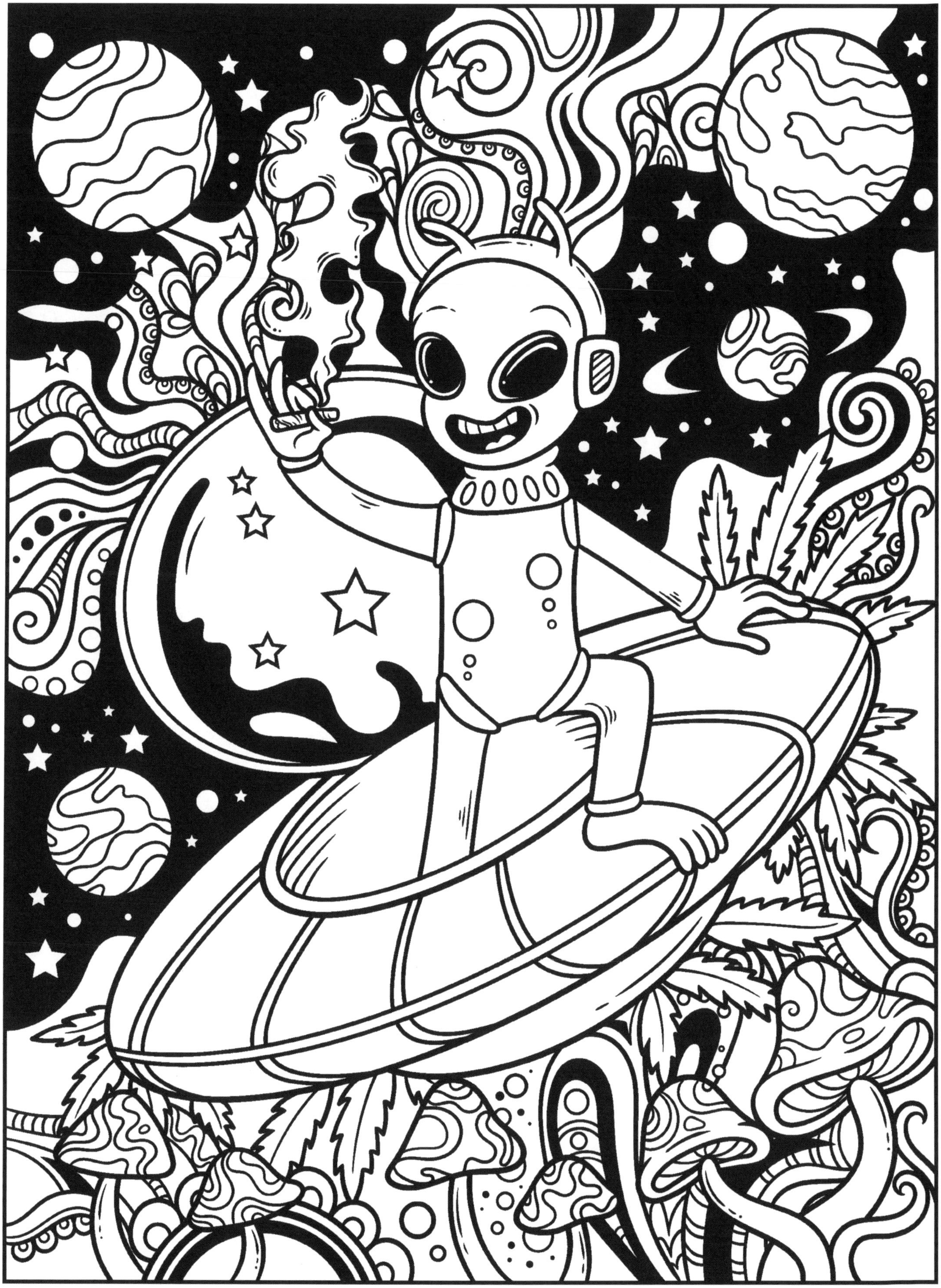

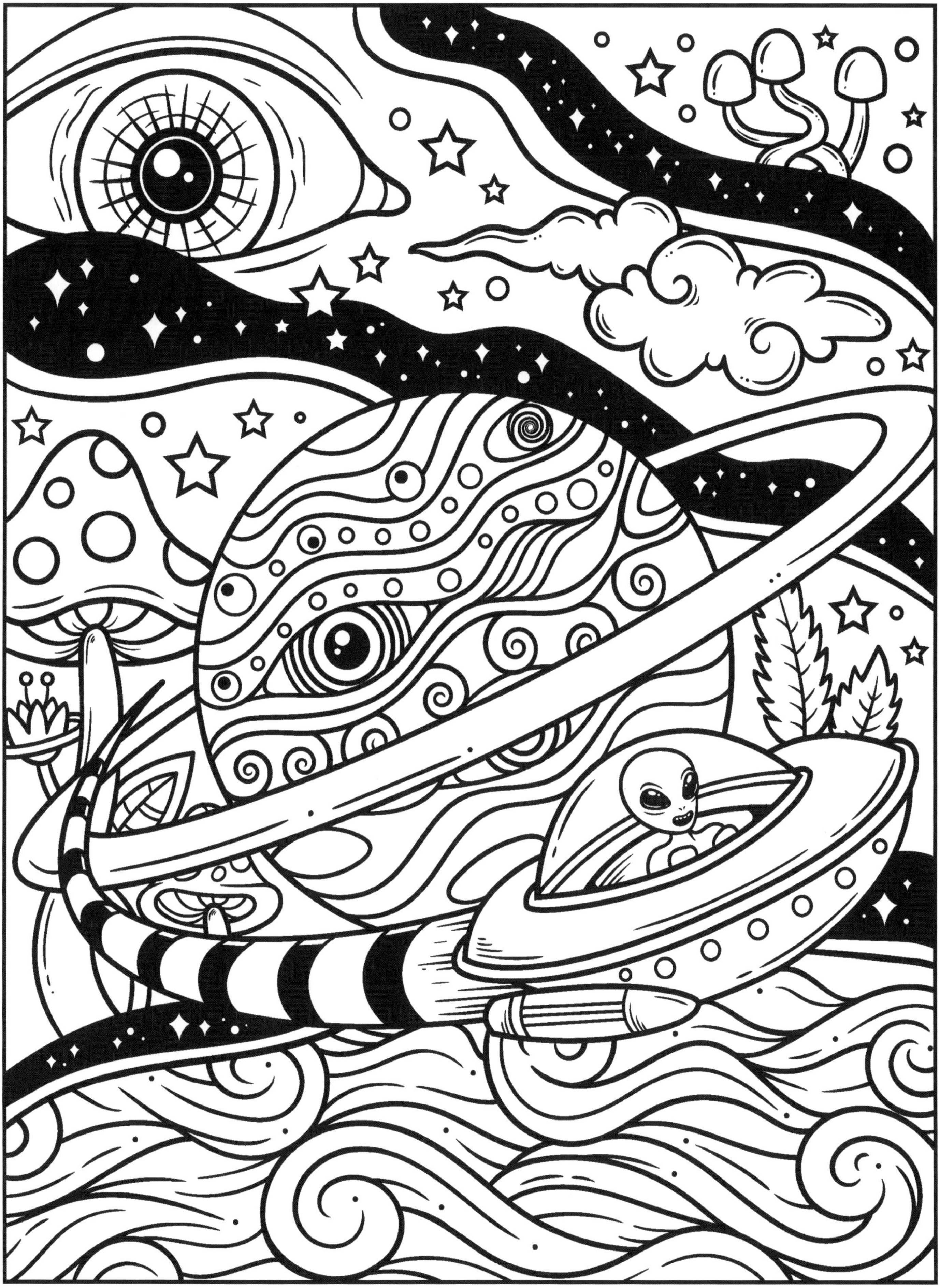

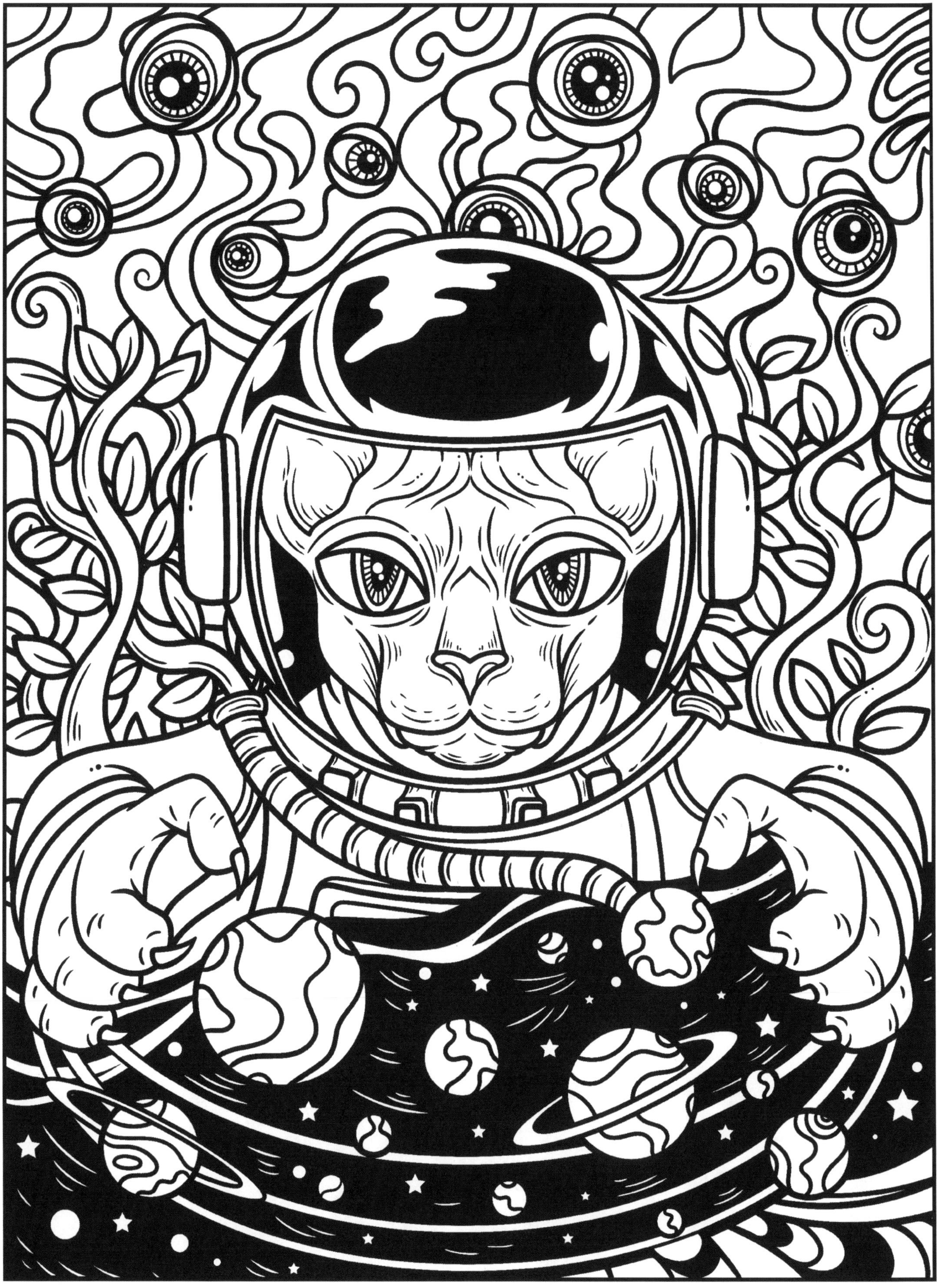

Made in the USA
Middletown, DE
01 December 2024

65827619R00029